Sally Fenton

A GIFT

OF

PRAYER

*The Spirituality
of Jewish Women*

Women of Reform Judaism / UAHC Press
633 Third Avenue
New York, NY 10017-6778

❧ Contents

List of Illustrations   7

Foreword   9

Acknowledgements   11

Prayers: *The Words of My Mouth*   17

For the Sabbath: *"The sweetness of Shabbat . . ."*   25

For Thanks and Blessing: . . . *Upon Seeing a Rainbow*   31

Meditations of Hope and Doubt: 37
 "The future is ours to create . . ."

Talking to God: *I Search*   43

Parents, Children, Grandchildren: 49
"May God help my children . . ."

In Response to Death: *For the Last Time*   57

Poems and Meditations: 65
"We sing of new beginnings every day . . ."

Contributors   73

✣ List of Illustrations

Prayers
Page 15   Untitled   Computer Graphic   Karen Weintraub
©Karen Weintraub

For the Sabbath
Page 23   "Shabbat Malkah II"   Papercut   Rose Ann Chasman
©Rose Ann Chasman

For Thanks and Blessing
Page 30   "The Blessing"   Mixed Media   Peter Langguth
©Peter Langguth

Meditations of Hope and Doubt
Page 35   "Yom Kippur"   Mosaic   Jonathan Mandell
©Jonathan Mandell

Talking to God
Page 42   "Hannah"   Painting with Gold Pigment   Sara Novenson
©Sara Novenson

Parents, Children, Grandchildren
Page 48   "The Family at Chanukah"   Oil on Canvas
Lynne Feldman   ©Lynne Feldman

In Response to Death

Page 55   "Rivers Meeting"   Glicée Print   Sara Novenson

©Sara Novenson

Poems and Meditations

Page 63   Untitled   Computer Graphic   Karen Weintraub

©Karen Weintraub

✒ Foreword

What are the prayers that women pray? The meditations of their hearts? Women of Reform Judaism, The Federation of Temple Sisterhoods, has been collecting the spiritual writings of Jewish women and their women clergy for over 50 years. Excerpts from their two latest books of prayers, poems and meditations, *Covenant of the Heart* (1993) and *Covenant of the Soul* (2000), are collected here.

This is a gift book, a gift of personal prayers, poetry, reflections, meditations for every occasion in a woman's life. In it, women guide and inspire us; they share their hopes and doubts with us—and with God. Women grope for understanding . . . rejoice at the birth of a grandchild . . . say a blessing on seeing a rainbow. They speak to women of all faiths who need the comfort, understanding and celebration expressed here that can help us through every occasion, every life-cycle event, every "ordinary" day. Here Jewish women reveal to *all* women—and to men—the struggles, the crises, the joys that all of us face.

The works of art throughout this volume depict prayer—prayer evoked by the majesty of nature, prayer that is integral to Jewish ritual, prayer inspired by awe of the Divine. Women of Reform Judaism has a long history of showcasing Jewish artists in the *WRJ Art Calendar*, making our members aware of Jewish art and collectors of it, and encouraging artists to reflect on Jewish themes. *A Gift of Prayer* includes artists whose work has appeared in the *WRJ Art Calendar* over the years. They have not "illustrated" the texts, but worked independently, responding to their own impulses of heart and soul. The result is a gift of words and art for every woman.

✒ Acknowledgements

A Gift of Prayer could not have been published without the work and participation of many individuals, whose help we gratefully acknowledge:

- The editorial review teams of *Covenant of the Heart* and *Covenant of the Soul*, who chose the selections to include from those submitted by Sisterhoods all over the world.
- The joint WRJ / UAHC Press committee that selected personal prayers from the two earlier books to include in the present one.
- The presidents of the National Federation of Temple Sisterhoods (NFTS) and Women of Reform Judaism (WRJ), Judith M. Hertz and Judith Silverman, during whose terms of office, and with whose support and encouragement, *Covenant of the Heart* and *Covenant of the* Soul appeared; Eleanor R. Schwartz, NFTS Executive Director Emeritus, who initiated the first project, and Ellen Y. Rosenberg, whose leadership brought both books—and this one—to publication.
- Editors Rabbi Susan Marks, who prepared the manuscript of *Covenant of the Heart*, and Eve F. Roshevsky, who edited *Covenant of the Heart, Covenant of the Soul* and *A Gift of Prayer, and* Shira Laskin, who assisted with the editorial work on the present volume.

- UAHC Press Managing Editor Stuart Benick, who supervised production of the book.
- Artists Camille Kress, Peter Langguth, Sara Novenson, Rose Ann Chassen, Lynne Feldman, Jonathan Mandell, and Karen Weintraub (who also contributed the cover art), who shared their talents and helped to make *A Gift of Prayer* not just a work of words, but one of art, as well.

A Gift of Prayer

🌿 Prayers
"The Words of My Mouth"

Let our lips sing the song
>That bursts from the heart.

A song of love for those who are near,
A song of cheer for the sick and needy,
A song of friendship for the lost and lonely,
A song of praise for You, O God.
Hear the strains drifting on the wind
>Of song and prayers
>>for the embattled countries.

And people too down-trodden to sing their song,
Or pray their prayers to You.
O God, show compassion so each can sing
>A new song of hope in this troubled world.

Based on parashat Terumah

Today, *Adonai*, we bring you our gifts:
Not precious metals, brightly colored textiles, animal skins, spices, oil or precious stones.
Instead, we bring You gifts of heart, of mind, of spirit, as well as the work of our hands.
We bring you the compassion we show to our families, to our friends, to those in need.
We bring you the gifts of intellect, the study of Torah, of Talmud, of our tradition.
We bring you the gifts of faith in our power to change things, of hope that, one day, this will be the world You wanted to create.
Adonai, please accept these, our gifts, and establish the work of our hands.

THE MONTH OF SHEVAT

In Israel, slender green shoots are beginning to push their way to the sun. Tight buds of flowers and trees begin to swell in anticipation of the coming Spring. This is a time of hope and promise.

I lift my heart to the Source of Life, to the One who nourishes and sustains all living things. As I observe the rebirth of life with the coming of Spring, may I too be reborn. Remove from me all thoughts, feelings, memories and desires that do not contribute to my positive growth. Help me to accept those things in my life that cause me difficulty. Teach me to deal with them creatively and successfully. Strengthen those ideas, feelings and desires that are life affirming, positive and beneficial to me. Help me to experience the world with a sense of awe and joy. I praise and thank You, Blessed Creator, the One Who nurtures and loves me.

God, Creator, grant us wisdom
"In these times that try men's souls."
Let our quest for understanding
Give us purpose, show us goals.
Help us now to lift the fallen,
Feed the hungry, free the slave.
Let us guide the blind, the crippled,
Keep us steadfast, make us brave.
You are wise where we are simple.
We are blind but You can see.
Help us then, O God of justice
As we lift our hearts to Thee.

THE WORDS OF MY MOUTH

An invitation to prayer

We sit in community
Elbow to elbow, eye to eye.
So close we brush against one another
as we move in prayer.
Ears filled with the voice of a friend, teacher, fellow traveler
      who prays with us from the next seat,
        from across the room.

We come to silence.
Rhythm of words, shared melody,
hushed.
Connected first one to one to all,
      We now let go.
To be alone.
To speak in mind
and heart
and soul
but not with lips.
One by one,
A miracle.

For what shall we pray?

Let us ask that we be cheerful, kind and friendly,

That we seek the good in all, the enmity in none,

That we try never to criticize, make no promise we cannot keep,

That we be loyal to our Temple and to our friends,

That we be calm in time of trouble, think before we speak,

hold onto our temper when things go wrong,

And every day by word and deed, in some unselfish way,

      may we try

to make someone happy.

And may the Almighty help us see our prayers answered.

Dear God,

Give us the strength to empower

ourselves and all women,

The wisdom to educate our people

and all people,

And the compassion to enlighten

our world.

לכה דודי לקראת כלה
פני שבת נקבלה

❧ For the Sabbath
"The sweetness of Shabbat . . ."

We reach for You, our God
from our quiet places.
May we stand still,
for a brief moment, and
listen to the rain—
Stand still, for a brief
moment, and watch the
play of sunlight and
shadow on the leaves.
For a brief moment—
listen to the world.

Let us stop the wheels
of every day to be aware of
Shabbat. Find the stillness
of the sanctuary
which the soul cherishes.
Renew the Covenant
of an ancient people.

We need a quiet
space to test the balance
of our days. The weight
of our own needs
against the heaviness
of the world's demands.
The balance is
precarious—steady
us with faith.

Quiet places and
stillness—where we will
hear our own best
impulses speak.
Quiet places and
stillness—from which
we will reach out to
each other.

We will find
strength in silence
and with this
strength we will
turn again to your
service.

L'CHA DODI

You can feel
          the Shabbat coming
Pungent odors
          fill the air.
Mothers all about
          are shouting,
"Clean the floors
          Prepare, prepare.
Polish the
          brass candlesticks,
Set the table,
          comb your hair."
The Sabbath bride
          approaches now,
Erasing every
          weekly care.

Slender curves,
my fingers touch the cool patina,
filled to the brim with the sweetness of Shabbat.

This graceful, silver cup,
raised to our lips, once reflected the faces of our
loved ones under a *chuppah*.

Drop by drop, a vessel of life,
filled with the poignant memories of rich tradition.

Not alone,
daughters and sons adding the beauty and innocence
of youth,
Tears of joy and sadness,
Almost to overflowing.

This graceful, silver cup,
once touched by the hands of those no longer with us,
Their gentle and loving legacy is not forgotten.

Slender curves, my fingers touch the cool patina,
filled to the brim with the sweetness of Shabbat.
Our cup of life.

This light is mine,
It was given to me in love,
It was given to me in Peace.
This light was hers,
That mother in our past
Who held it with pride.
This light was theirs,
Those sisters of ages past
Who held it in awe.
This light will be theirs,
Those daughters of our heart,
May they hold it with care.
A light won by strength,
by suffering,
      by selflessness.
We praise You, Oh God.
And pray that for all time

We will kindle our light
With blessed freedom.
The flame a constant,
A beacon in our lives.

✌ For Thanks and Blessing
Upon Seeing a Rainbow

Dear God, a prayer of thanksgiving is sometimes difficult. I want it to come from the heart. I want it to be sincere. But, I am often consumed with my own small needs of the moment and I fail to appreciate what only You could have created and given to us.

I must reach deep inside for just a moment. I must ask myself: What is the essence of my life? Is it what is happening to me tomorrow, or can I appreciate time in a broader sense? Are my possessions too great a priority? Have I done my share of giving to others since last Shabbat?

This is why I take a moment to reflect before I offer You my thanks for all the gifts bestowed upon me.

I am thankful for You, God everlasting, from whom I draw strength every day. I am thankful for all of my family, whose ties mean so much. I am forever thankful for the comfort of my friends and the joy they add to my life. You have put us in a most beautiful world of which I could never tire—the animals, the plants, the stars in the sky. And lastly, I am most grateful for the gift of being a Jew, for the ability to study and ask why, for the gift of Your Torah.

From my heart, *Adonai*, I thank you.

A BLESSING UPON SEEING A RAINBOW

Dear God!
How good of you to bring me a rainbow
on such a miserable day!
Just when my sorrows were mounting,
and everything looked so gray,
You surprised me with your wonder,
and gave me a brilliant display!

B'ruchah At, Shechinah, Malkat HaOlam, zokheret ha-b'rit
v'ne'emanah bi-v'ritah v'kayemet b'ma'amarah.

Blessed are You, *Shechinah*, Queen of the Universe, Who
remembers the Covenant and keeps faith with the people Israel.

Creator of the galaxies, You rule the infinitudes of space yet allow us
to feel the wonder of Your presence in our inner selves.

Help us, who cannot truly comprehend You, to be worthy partners in
Your creation.
Hear our prayers of praise, supplication and aspiration.

Bless the leaders and members of our congregation. Teach us to serve
our temple, community, the Jewish people, Israel and humankind.

Thus may we more surely honor You.

Blessing of the children

May you know God as Abraham our father did, and
    face your trials with great dignity

Like our mother Sarah, may you be gracious and kind
    to those who pass your way

May you be as gentle as Isaac and as determined
    as Rebecca

Like Jacob, may you be dedicated and conscientious
    in all you set out to do

May you be blessed, as Leah was blessed, with a close
    and loving family

And like Rachel, may you radiate warmth from your soul
    to everyone whose life touches yours.

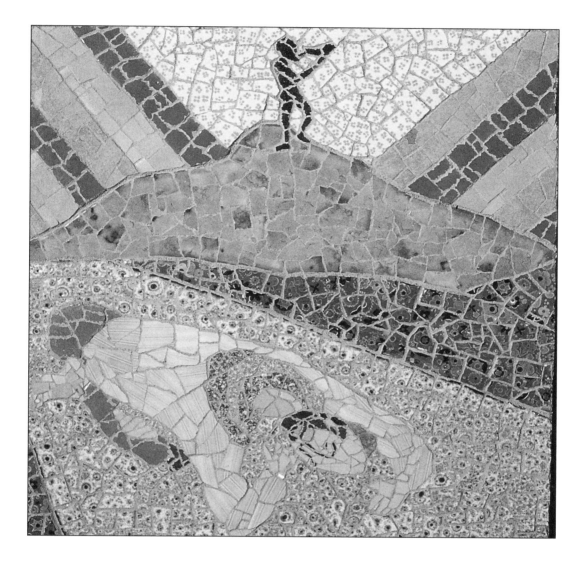

❧ Meditations of Hope and Doubt
"The Future is Ours to Create . . ."

The future is ours to create—
What a terrifying thought!
Who are we to be entrusted
    with such a mission,
    such a challenge,
    such a responsibility?
How do we know what to do?
Where do we start?
We call upon our heritage—
Rich and embracing,
Filled with love and support
Never defeating, always reassuring.
It strengthens us in mind, body and soul.
Foremost in our thoughts—
Not to disappoint those who came before us,
Those who sanctioned us with the precept
    to do what is right,
    to help those in need,
    to be sensitive to the feelings of others,
    to refrain from hurting anyone.
The future is ours to create—
What an exhilarating prospect!

What a challenge!
What a responsibility!
God, help us to know what to do.
Guide us,
Nurture our strength and
Sustain our courage.

We ponder the past
We think about the future:
Where have we been?
Where are we now?
What is the connection?

What heritage did I receive from my parents?
What will I bequeath to my children
        (and grandchildren)?
What gifts have I received from my brothers, my sisters,
        my friends?
What can I give to others?
Where do my people, my community fit in my life?

If I can make someone's life better,
I will not regret the past.
If I can help someone grow,
I will not fear the future.

Oh God, let me make some mark on this world,
Let me create some image,
Let me leave some memory of myself.
If only even for an instant—
Let someone think or say:
The world is better because I passed this way.

I was told You didn't exist;
I was told You couldn't exist;
There was no science to You.
But You burst across my soul
You were what I lived
And what I breathed,
 You are what I am
And who I am

The blending emotion and rationality
Reasonable tears and unreasonable laughter
Wild hopelessness and unquenchable hope

I have no choice but life
Because of You.

In penitence, I seek God's will.
The errors of human emotions
Lie heavy upon me.
Their grievous burden bends my neck.
I look inward and see fault.
I reach outward and ask pardon.
I gaze upward and know hope.

I find no comfort in old places
But new ones are untried, elusive.
Solace escapes my grasp, replaced by questions.
To understand God's will
Separate from my own wants.
I long for a strong arm
Sweeping me inexorably in the right way.

Instead I feel tiny tuggings at my mind,
Uncertainties abounding.
This road, that path?
I do not know.

I open my heart, straining to answer God's call.
I bare my soul, striving to know God's will.
I am weak and want to be free of this burden.
It stays with me still,
To be lifted not by me but by God,
In God's time, to God's purpose.

I grope for understanding.
Needing its light to lead me from
The darkness of my own making.
Who can comprehend my searchings,
My pitiful answers to questions dimly perceived?
What influences in my world can sway me?
In others' words do I hear God's voice
Or only that of my own longings?

In repentance, I know God's will.
The errors of human emotions
Are lifted from me,
Their grievous burden gone from my neck.
I looked inward and found strength.
I reached outward and received love.
I gazed upward and discovered truth.

❧ Talking to God
"I Search"

Creator of courage and love
may I be blessed
with strength and health
I want to light up the lives
of the people I love and meet

The rising of the sun reminds me of
the essence of my mother
the aura of the one whose name
I carry
May my light shine forth like theirs
And when I die, *Shechinah*,
don't let my light go out.

Wonder of all wonders, as trees grow and reach toward the sky, allow me to reach and grow in my life.

As your creation sheds its leaves, let me shed the hardness of my heart and soul.

As trees rest in the winter in order to grow again in the spring, allow me to take the time to rest in order that I, too, may bloom and grow again.

Dear God,
Help us to maintain our sense of humor.
In our lives we have promised to help "repair the world"
yet daily we encounter destruction, hatred, and threat
    on a worldwide basis.
Even our own personal situations sometimes
overwhelm us.

Help us to remember that You are a lover of laughter.
We can laugh with our friends or at ourselves,
and in so doing, lighten our hearts so we can face
another day.

Sense of humor is a precious attribute of humanity.
    You gave it to us.
Help us to see its purpose, and to cherish it.

God, often I think
You are the only One who listens to me.

That's enough.

Courage
Adonai, bless me with courage
        Help me gain strength from You
Life has a way of handing us surprises
        to be overcome
Create in me a clear and steady focus
        a heart that is filled with the awareness that
        Adonai is with me
                on the sunniest day and in the darkest night
I will be whatever life demands of me
Courage is my knowledge of You.

I SEARCH

Dearest God,
I can't say the words today.
They are beautiful and clear in my *siddur*.
But this day, I somehow can't say them.
I long for knowledge of You, for nearness to You,

But I can't say the words.
Responsive readings and prescribed prayer do not sit
on my tongue today.
I find no *kavanah* when I rise to praise You, to declare
Your oneness.
I am in the congregation, but not of the congregation.
My eyes wander to the window, my thoughts to the ordinary.
Do you read my silence, hear the whirl of my thought?
You must. I know you do.
For at this moment, I feel as close to You
As if I sat at the foot of the very throne of Heaven.

Dear God,

I am writing this letter because I often find it difficult to communicate with You in other, more traditional ways. You do not spring easily out of the pages of my prayerbook, nor do You float ethereally among the arched ceilings in my Temple. When I call Your name, I hear no voice responding to my own.

Would our relationship be different if I knew You on a daily basis? As it is, I seem to think of You only in times of crisis or joy. Would I feel closer to You if I turned to You at times other than when I am afraid and pleading for Your help? I do praise You in my head in rare moments of euphoria when I am especially touched by the miracle of the world You have created. Yet, this is not enough. I know there can be much more between us.

At times I have felt a great intimacy with You. It is clear, warm and all encompassing. But this sensation dissipates like a dream that fades the longer I am awake. I try to recapture that feeling but only a memory remains and it too grows dim.

I am seeking renewal. Fill my soul with the breath of Your magnificence. Surround me with Your goodness and love. Rejuvenate me so that I may have the strength to reach out to others and revitalize them. This is my prayer, now and forevermore.

Sincerely yours,

Parents, Children, Grandchildren

"May God help my children . . ."

ADDITIONS TO THE *SH'MA*

With all my heart, with all my soul, with all my might,
I pray for the health of this child.
I pray for it to be perfect in mind and body,
To issue safely and easily from me
    at the proper time,
To grow steadily and sturdily
In a home filled with joy at its presence,
To be nurtured into a person who greets the world
with passion, enthusiasm, dance, love, humility, faith.

With all my heart, with all my soul, with all my might,
I pray for the health of this world.
I beg its leaders to temper their insanity with reason,
So that my child may be born into a world that seeks
    longevity, not annihilation.
Let the world join in the thrill of creation,
And turn its back on the lust for destruction.
Let my child never know the pain and absurdity
    of warfare.
Let it take part in the dances of peace.

With all my heart, with all my soul, with all my might,
I pray for God to watch over me and my family,
I pray for strength and courage when I labor to
    bring forth this child,
I pray for the capacity to return my husband's great
    love for me,
I pray for the ability to love and nurture this child,
I pray to feel God's presence now and always.

FOR ADOPTION

I sit in dim light, watching my
daughter sleep. She is beautiful, this
child who is of the flesh of another,
who has made me the mother I did not
think I would be.

My eyes turn heavenward as I give
thanks: thanks to a young girl I will
never know, thanks to a Nurturing Spirit
that has watched over me and brought
me to this life.

Thank you, God.

FOR PARENTS AND GRANDPARENTS

First comes love, a soul mate who shares life's vision,
the completion of oneself.
Then come children, the joy of giving life to
the next generation,
The *mitzvah* of being fruitful and multiplying
realized in a soft bundle of humanity.
The trials of nurturing are matched by fulfillment,
watching the flowering of new souls, guiding them
through the early years of adulthood.

The cycle continues, with children searching to find
their own way, guided by God's teachings and our examples.
And, if we are blessed, with children finding their own
soul mates.

Soon, the utter joy of a child's child in my arms,
God's blessing realized in a tiny shape nestled close to
me and boring into a special place in my heart. Peace
and contentment.

Thank you, God, for Your blessings.

May God help my children to choose a life of personal satisfaction and fulfillment.

May each find an interest—a passion—to work and strive for.

May each find a partner with whom to share life so together they are stronger than individually.

May each listen to their heart and find love and joy in life.

May God watch over my children and bless them.

FOR MY DAUGHTERS

Nine months of dreaming led to you
Each unique, yet part of me
Glorious mornings brought you forth
With joy and struggle, pain and ecstasy
Each of you has changed my life.
An indelible stamp—love unconditional—
Has seared my soul as I've watched you grow.
Pride, love, and respect for you deepen and twine together
Daily I think of each of you—
Are you well? Are you happy?
Have I done all I could to prepare you for life's challenges?
For you, my daughters, I pray… I wish upon the stars at night
May God protect you every moment of every day
May the heritage of our people be with you
May you be like Miriam and Ruth and Deborah
May you love your partners and your someday children
May your love for each other strengthen as your lives lengthen
And, my daughters, may you know forever that you are the love, the joy of my life.

Our bearded son
stands under the canopy
not touching her hand
but touching
even so
in rented
pearl grey
only the back of his head
looks familiar
and his resonant voice
saying
I will
in this time
of their beginning
his father and I
spread open our hands
as we must
watching him leave
as he must
he travels east
of where we stand
waving
his step and her step
sure-footed
moving together
as our hands
overflowing
cup the nectar
and brine
of letting him go

In Response to Death

"For the Last Time"

The ancient words
I don't understand them
They are in a language
I do not know

Why are they so familiar?
There is a rhythm to them
a beat, a pulse I understand
From somewhere very deep inside me
My heart, my soul
I am connected to a past I never lived
and to a future I shall not know

A member of the human race
Running through my time
And still, connected to many lives which came before me
so many cultures, faces
tears and joys

A Jew, connected
To the past, to a future
Hoping always

That peace and love will finally come to all the world
That we may really live with no barriers
And each of us, in the comfort and beauty of
       our varied traditions

Long before I understood what it means to be Jewish
I knew that I was part of something
larger than myself
beyond my comprehension

The *Kaddish* reminds me every week
of my family, and my friends
my people, and all the people of the world
the living, and those who live on in our hearts and minds
of the earth, and all its creatures
of God's universe
And it is a reminder of my responsibility
to fulfill the promise of peace
while I am on earth
Shalom

FOR THE LAST TIME

How do you know
when it's the last time?
The last time to ask
"How are you?

How was your day?"
The last time to say
"I love you.
Good night . . . sweet dreams."

You don't.
And so you must reach out
with love and compassion
at every opportunity
to show those who love you
that you care
you love
and need to be needed . . .
in a world where you suddenly find yourself
alone once again
in an achingly painful way
because someone you love
has left you behind
to seek your own paths
and truths
in an uncertain place.

The only thing certain
is that you're not truly alone
because of those who do love you
and for that be thankful
and grateful
and feel blessed
that you were able to say
"Good night . . . I love you"
one last time.

I HAD A FRIEND

I had a friend. Graceful
as a bird against the sky.
He flew high.
I felt the wind
as he spread his wings
while I soared alongside.
He is gone. Fallen to earth,
as the dust.
But I still feel
the rush of the breeze
which lifted me to greater heights,
because I had a friend.

KADDISH MEDITATION

Whenever death comes, it is too soon for those of us left to mourn. When death leaves adults to grieve over parents or grandparents, aged aunts or older siblings, it is an imponderable anguish, but we bow to God's plan. Yet when death comes too soon, wounding parents who will never see their children grown, hurting children too young to understand, or spouses who ache for just one more hug, it can seem that God has abandoned us.

But death and our pain are as much a part of life as are our joys and strivings.

To live is to be touched by death.

May we always remember to reach out to those who mourn, and never to forsake God who has given us life.

We are sisters
when we communicate
with the warmth
of a word and a smile.
We are sisters
when we share
the bitterness of tears
the crystal joy of merriment.
We are sisters
when one of us is gone
and all of us
are desolate.
May those we honor
with our prayers
live on in our memories
and our lives.

❧ Poems and Meditations

"We sing of new beginnings
every day . . ."

At the shore of the Red Sea, Miriam took up her timbrel
      and sang her song: a song of praise to God.
With confidence and love, she led our ancestors
      through their fear and hesitation,
      until all hands were joined,
      all voices raised in hymn and thanksgiving.
May her example lead us, too, and may her song
      soon grow to be truly ours:
The song of women and men joined in understanding and respect.
The song of God's miracles: an earth protected and cherished,
      a gift for our children and the generations to come.
The song of a land once ravished by war, now quiet and content,
      her soldiers home, to leave no more.
The songs of a world redeemed: The song of peace.

❧

The Hasidic Rabbi Zusya taught his disciples that they must be the best of themselves. He said, "When I go to life eternal, God will not ask me, 'Why were you not Moses?' God will ask me, "Why were you not Zusya?'"

We sing of new beginnings every day,
Each in our time to praise in deeds and dreams
The wonder of life, God's work in all our ways.
We gather in the scattered, radiant beams.
Moses did not see the promised land
Expanding new horizons round the bend.
His task to lead a slave-accustomed band
To march toward freedom, searchers without end.
Can I do my share, each day we ask,
Mindful of the past, building for tomorrow.
Not Moses, nor Zusya, nor any borrowed mask.
To be ourselves today, this road we furrow.
Ours not to end the work, nor even start,
Ours to give each day a willing heart.

Noisy days, busy days, phone ringing days,
     children call, husbands ask, cars stall.
(Where in this world is the moment of knowing?)
TV's blast, walkman's squawk, dog's bark
(Where in ourselves is the moment of growing?)

Praise be to God for the ordinary day,
     when each minute is filled,
When each moment demands.
Praise be to God for the day without pain,
     when our loved ones are well,
When we walk hand in hand.
Give me the strength to appreciate life,
     when the day is not special,
An everyday day.
When we sink with exhaustion
     from a day's work well met,
Pray for the chance that we
     do better yet.

I AM

I am a woman.
Able, capable, unfulfilled,
Eloquent, sure, yet questioning—
Nurturer, mother, wife,
Homemaker, breadwinner, student, politician.
Humble, soft, compliant,
Yet proud, strong, defiant—
I am a Woman.

I am a Jew.
Probing, questioning, accepting.
Is there a personal God?
Is there a need for a Jewish State?
Am I my sister's keeper?
Humble, soft, compliant,
Yet proud, strong, defiant—
I am a Jew.

I am an American.
Searching for answers—what are the questions?
Democracy, motherhood, apple pie,
Sex on TV, violence, searching for peace.
But here the people speak—is anyone listening?
Humble, soft, compliant,
Yet proud, strong, defiant—
I am an American.

I am an American Jewish woman.
I hope, I dream. I believe.
Part of a strong heritage, producer of change.
There is a place for Peace, there is a place for Love.
There is God.
Humble, soft, compliant,
Yet proud, strong, defiant—
I am an American Jewish Woman.

TO A DREAMER

Some dreams are of things past,
Warm and wonderful,
Or sad, or frightening,
When we wake from them
We shake them off.
Some dreams are in the present,
Shutting out the world around us
And letting us drift on a cloud
More real than reality.
And what about the future,
The dreams that are creative,
Imaginative, seeds of events to come?
Those dreams don't deal
With nostalgia or fear,
Nor do they keep us
Suspended in time or space,
But they propel us into action.
We need them. We need all three.
We need the dreamers.
Pity the minds that do not dream.

Sing of Jewish women then and now:
Celebrate the women of the Book—
        the matriarchs and the judges.
Honor the dreamers.
Sing of Jewish women then and now:
Praise the women of the home—
the nurturers and the enablers.
Hallow the builders.
Sing of Jewish women then and now:
Salute the women of the world—
        the leaders and the laborers.
Exalt the doers.
Sing the silence, sing of strength
Songs of pride, songs of joy.
Sing of Jewish women then and now:
        Heroines all.

A COVENANT OF THE SOUL

Deep within, deep within
Our mothers guarded a sacred promise:
they would teach with ageless wisdom,
they would nurture with silent strength,
they would heal with courageous love.
We, who are their daughters, traverse bridges of time.
We gaze into the past to see ourselves.

Now we possess their eternal pledge:
A covenant of the soul.

We, who are teachers, build eternal bridges.
Guiding through our deeds,
shaping with our hands,
touching with our dreams.
Each moment overflows with insight, with creativity,
with passion.

We, who are nurturers, protect eternal bridges.
We are shield and shelter, shepherding with confidence,
allowing heartsongs to soar and embraced souls to reach.
Each moment overflows with comfort, with sustenance,
with freedom.

We, who are healers, repair eternal bridges.
Whispering of desire and hope, weaving together lifeprayers,
risking love.
Divine sparks refill shattered vessels.
Each moment overflows with bravery, with spirit,
with trust in ourselves and in God.
We, who are their daughters, renew our faith
in their solemn oath:
A covenant of the soul.

Each of our moments overflows with blessing.
We are the guarantors of the promise.
The journey continues through us.
The journey continues through us.

ME
MY FAMILY
THE JEWISH PEOPLE
AND TORAH, A TREE OF LIFE
ROOTS HOLDING ON TO THE PAST
BRANCHES REACHING TO THE FUTURE
LEAVES DANCING LIKE CHILDREN
GROWING AND CHANGING
WITH THE SEASONS
TEACHING:
PEACE
CARING
SHARING
TOLERANCE
UNDERSTANDING
FROM PARENT TO CHILD
FROM GENERATION TO GENERATION

Contributors

PRAYERS

"Let our lips sing the song . . ."   17
Hanna G. Stein
New York, NY

"Today, *Adonai*, we bring you our gifts . . . "   18
Lee Egerton
Baltimore, MD

The Month of Shevat   19
Rabbi Jo David
New York, NY

"God, Creator, grant us wisdom . . ."   19
Margie Lipman
Dallas, TX

The Words of My Mouth   20
Rabbi Debra R. Hachen
Westborough, MA

"Dear God, give us the strength . . ."   21
Diane Kaplan
Minneapolis, MN

"For what shall we pray . . ."   21
Shirley Robinson (z'l)
Cae Town, South Africa

FOR THE SABBATH

"We reach for You, our God . . ."   25
 Priscilla R. Stern (z'l')
Great Barrington, MA

L'cha Dodi   27
Harriet G. Epstein
Falls Church, VA

"Slender curves, my fingers touch the cool patina . . ."   28
Marion Frankel
Mississauga, Ontario, CN

"This light is mine . . ."   29
Alison Lurie
Stockton, CA

FOR THANKS AND BLESSING

"Dear God, a prayer of thanksgiving . . . "   31
Debbi Mandel
San Antonio, TX

Blessing Upon Seeing a Rainbow   32
Jan Poscovsky
Missouri City, TX

"Creator of the Galaxies . . ."   33
Jane Evans
New Rochelle, NY

"May you know God as Abraham . . ." 33
Rabbi Leah Kroll
Los Angeles, CA

MEDITATIONS OF HOPE AND DOUBT

"The future is ours to create . . ." 37
Ellen Y. Rosenberg
Riverdale, NY

"We ponder the past . . ." 38
Judith M. Hertz
New York, NY

"I was told You didn't exist..."   39
Susie Bayer
New York, NY

"In penitence, I seek God's will . . ." 40
Carole J. Cook
Indianapolis, IN

TALKING TO GOD

"Creator of courage and love . . ." 43
Emita Levy
New York, NY

"Dear God, help us to maintain our sense of humor . . ." 44
Francine Kolin
New York, NY

"Wonder of all wonders . . ." 45
Paula C. Yablonsky
Schenectady, NY

"God, often I think . . ."   45
Janet Caro Murphy
Dallas, TX

Courage   45
Anita Moise Rosefield Rosenberg
Charleston, SC

I Search   46
Esther Saritzky
Northridge, CA

"Dear God, I am writing this letter . . . "   47
Randee Friedman
San Diego, CA

PARENTS, CHILDREN, GRANDCHILDREN

Additions to the *Sh'ma*   49
Rabbi Judy Shanks
Oakland, CA

For Adoption   50
Patricia Nacht
Merrick, NY

For Parents and Grandparents   51
Judith Silverman
Yarmouthport, MA

"May God help my children . . ."   52
Helene H. Waranch
Baltimore, MD

For My Daughters   52
Rosanne Selfon
Lancaster, PA

"Our bearded son . . ." 53
Naomi Spigle
South Bend, IN

IN RESPONSE TO DEATH

"The ancient words . . ." 57
Emily Dina Ruth Maltz
Minneapolis, MN

For the Last Time 58
Robin Fox
Fresno, CA

I Had a Friend 59
Betty Benson
Stonybrook, NY

Kaddish Meditation 60
Debra R. Darvick
Bloomfield Hills, MI

"We are sisters . . ." 61
Doris Panoff
Boston, MA

POEMS AND MEDITATIONS

"At the shore of the Red Sea . . ." 65
Rabbi Elyse Goldstein
Concord, Ontario, CN

"We sing of new beginnings every day . . ." 66
Norma U. Levitt
Monroe Township, NJ